Packaging, Warehousing, Transportation, Distribution, Blockchain, and Risk Management
In Action

Louis Bevoc and Allison Shearsett

Published by
NutriNiche System LLC

For information contact:
info@nutriniche.com

I0490707

Louis Bevoc books...simple explanations of complex subjects

Packaging and Warehousing in Organizations

A Basic Introduction

Louis Bevoc

Published by
NutriNiche System LLC

For information contact:
info@nutriniche.com

Louis Bevoc books...simple explanations of complex subjects

Packaging

Warehousing

Packaging

Introduction

Most products purchased by people require some type of packaging. Based on this fact, it is not surprising that billions of dollars are spent annually on packaged products. Even exposed bulk items such as apples require packaging in the form of a bag to move the product from the location where it was purchased to the consumer's home. The bag is used to facilitate the transfer of the apples, but it also keeps them together and protects them from outside contamination. In other words, the bag has multiple reasons for being used....as do many other types of packages.

Below are major reasons that packaging is used for all types of products using grass fertilizer as an example for better understanding. Please note that these reasons are common-sense based and quite simple, but they are an important aspect of packaging that needs to be discussed.

Transportation

Many products need to be moved from one place to another, and packaging helps achieve this efficiently and effectively. Proper packaging enables people to transfer items in ways that could not be done without that packaging.

Example

Robert needs grass fertilizer for the lawn surrounding his house. He goes to a hardware store finds granulated fertilizer in ten-pound rigid plastic containers. He buys two containers, puts them in his car, and takes them to his house. The rigid plastic packaging allows him to transport the fertilizer in bulk with relative ease. If the product was not packaged, Robert would have to make several trips to the hardware store because he could not physically carry twenty pounds of granulated product in his hands.

Protection

This applies to people, the environment, and the products that are purchased. Packaging protects people and the environment from being harmed by the products it contains, and it protects the products it contains from damage caused by people or the environment.

Example

Packaging protects Robert from coming in contact with the fertilizer. This is important because exposure could cause his health to be adversely affected.

Packaging also prevents Robert from spilling the fertilizer in unwanted areas that could potentially damage natural environments. Additionally, packaging protects the fertilizer from damaging elements such as rain or snow, and it prevents Robert from accidentally mixing it with other products, chemicals, or materials that render it ineffective or create a hazard.

Information

Packaging contains valuable information regarding the product and its safety including:

Identification

Consumers want most things they purchase to be identified, and packaging provides a perfect opportunity for that identification.

Example

The name of the fertilizer is *All Purpose Lawn Fertilizer*. When people see this, they know it is an item that can be used on the grass around their homes.

Safety

This information expands upon product protection by letting consumers know if the product is safe for humans.

Example

Potential acute health effects for the grass fertilizer include:

Eye contact: Causes eye irritation.
Inhalation: Causes nose and lung irritation.
Skin contact: No known significant effects.
Ingestion: Harmful if swallowed. Causes lip, mouth, throat, and stomach irritation.

Price

Money is important to the vast majority of consumers, and price can influence their purchasing decision....regardless of their like for the product. Most packages contain pricing information that aids in the decision process.

Example

The granulated grass fertilizer containers have a price of $13.00 written on them. This price is not the most or least expensive compared to other fertilizers and is therefore considered mid-range.

Weight or volume

Consumers want to know the weight or volume of the products that they are purchasing so they can calculate the price per pound for a comparative analysis of similar products. Most packages contain this information in a prominently displayed area.

> *Example*
>
> The containers for the grass fertilizer have "Net Wt. 10 lbs (160 oz.)" written on them. Consumers know that the cost of one container is $13.00, so they can calculate the cost per pound to be $1.30 for comparison to other fertilizers.

Space

Space is critical for most retail outlets. They need to showcase and store a wide variety of products, including those that compete with each other, to attract customers and increase sales. Proper packaging configuration saves space by maximizing the number of products that can fit into a designated area.

Now you understand the basic reasons that packages are used. The next section expands on this discussion by examining the different types of packaging used by organizations for their products.

Types

Companies that sell products need to decide on the type of material(s) that they are going to use for the packaging of those products. Each type of packaging material has unique strengths and weaknesses, and testing and research are often required to select the best type for the job. In short, the type of packaging material selected depends on the need and application.

Three major types of packaging material are plastic, glass, and paper. The following describes each of these for better understanding:

Plastic

This packaging includes rigid and flexible plastic...both of which have a wide variety of uses. Plastic is advantageous because it is durable and lightweight. This makes it economical for transportation in addition to providing a high level of product protection. However, plastic packages are heavy polluters of the environment. They are a threat to many types of wild animals, and they typically take a long time to decompose. An example of rigid plastic is a drum used to contain chemicals, and an example of flexible plastic is a bottle used to contain water.

Glass

Glass packaging includes any container made of glass including bottles and jars. Glass is heavy and breakable, but it also makes an attractive package and is recyclable. Glass is typically not a big threat to wildlife, but it does take a long time to decompose. An example of a glass bottle is that used for beer, and an example of a glass jar is that used for jam or jelly.

Paper

Paper packaging typically includes paperboard, chipboard, corrugated, and paper. It is advantageous for heavy materials like appliances and meat, and it is typically recyclable and biodegradable. However, wet paper products are virtually useless and can create safety hazards. An example of paper packaging is that used to wrap artwork, an example of paperboard packaging is that used for wedding cakes, and an example of corrugated packaging is that used for automobile batteries.

Metal

Metal packaging typically includes aluminum and tin. It is advantageous due to the tamper-resistant barrier it provides. However, metal packages are usually thrown in the trash rather than recycled or returned for the deposit...and this is bad for the environment. An example of aluminum is a can used for soda pop, and an example of tin is a pressurized can used for foaming bathroom cleaner.

Now that you understand the basic types of packaging, let's discuss the role that packaging plays in marketing products....also known as the marketing purpose.

Marketing purpose

Packaging is used to protect products and the people who purchase them. However, packaging also plays a huge role in marketing. Packaging engineers, designers, and scientists work to develop packaging that gets "the most bang for the buck." The packages they develop consider many different factors, but they always consider the following for marketing purposes:

Attractiveness

It was a wise person who first said, "You never get a second chance at a first impression." This is true in life, and it has great application in packaging. People are attracted to products based on their impressions of those products, and that impression is driven by packaging.

Consumers use packaging to help them determine if a product is useful. In some cases, they do not need or want a product, but the packaging influences their decision to buy it. This does not make sense from a practical standpoint, but it does satisfy desires that people did not know they had until they came upon the product. This might sound crazy, but it happens on a fairly regular basis...and it is why companies invest large amounts of time and money into the packaging of their products.

In short, product packaging is a major factor in marketing because it appeals to consumers. They are attracted to what they see, and they spend their money to buy it. Without this attractiveness, products do not stand out and struggle to keep up with the competition.

Value

What is value? This is a challenging question to answer because value has a different meaning for everyone. However, packaging can add value for the majority of people simply by containing a few simple words. Examples include "on sale," "save 20 percent," or "buy one, get one free." These words increase value and lead to consumer purchases.

In terms of sales, value might be the most important aspect of packaging. Consumers want to save money, and the information on packages allows them to do so. This is the way it was in the past, the way it is now, and the way it will be in the future.

Practicality

In some ways, practicality is the opposite of attractiveness. Many consumers require the products they purchase to be protected, clean, sanitary, and environmentally responsible. If they trust the packaging of a product, then they are likely to buy it...and they are willing to pay more money for that product than they are for a similar product with packaging that they do not trust.

Practicality is a marketing factor that will most likely never go away. Consumers have basic needs for the products they purchase, and practical packaging meets those needs. It might not be fancy, but it serves an important purpose. In short, practicality refers to making sure packages function properly.

As you can see, packaging has a marketing purpose. It is driven by consumer demands, and it will change as those demands change. However, packaging of the future will be pressured by other factors to change....and those factors are discussed in the next section.

Future

People who are not directly involved in the packaging world probably do not think about it very much. After all, they make purchases for the product inside...not the surrounding packaging material. They usually do not notice that the packaging of a product is high quality because they expect it to be that way. However, they will notice a problem with the packaging very quickly if it does do what it is supposed to do. For example, a broken tamper-resistant seal on an aspirin bottle usually results in consumers refusing to buy that product. They will search for a good seal...or they will purchase the same product elsewhere.

It is rather obvious that the future of packaging rests on meeting consumer demands. However, other factors affecting the future are not so obvious. These factors include pressure from outside groups, government intervention, technology, and manufacturing costs. Please consider the following:

Technological advances

Technology affects virtually every aspect of organizations in some way, shape, or form...and packaging is no exception. Durability, strength, tear resistance, tamper resistance, oxygen permeability, and moisture permeability are all examples of packaging characteristics that have been impacted by technology. These features and many others will continue to improve with technological advancements, but the biggest impact will likely be the way these packages are manufactured after the advancements have been implemented.

The biggest manufacturing advancement in terms of technology will involve 3D printing. This process has the potential to completely transform the packaging world by printing materials on demand. At the moment, 3D printing is too costly to be used the majority of packaging manufacturers to utilize it properly. However, like any other new technology, the price will get lower and the technology will improve in the future. When that happens, watch out because companies will use this process in many different ways...including individualizing packaging for the masses. This might sound impossible, but it is not. It will happen, and it not that far off.

Consumer demands

This book makes it clear that packaging design is consumer-driven, and this will not change in the future. However, consumer demands will increase making it more challenging for organizations that use packaging for their products. Consumers will want to know more about the products they are purchasing, and that information will need to come on the package. Consumers will also demand more in terms of safety. They will want to be assured that the products they are purchasing are safe to use or consume....and packaging plays a big role in that safety.

Regulatory intervention

Along the same lines as consumer demands, regulatory agencies will also require more from packaging. For example, food sold to the general public will require more detailed ingredient statements and nutritional facts panels. All ingredients will need to be listed with nothing hidden from the consumer, and more nutritional information will be required.

There will also be more regulations regarding the chemical make-up of packaging materials. Any material considered to be carcinogenic or dangerous in any way to people's health will be banned.

Last, but certainly not least, physical packaging standards will be implemented. Strength testing will be required to assure packaging material can hold up under normal conditions. For example, a corrugated box for a 50 lb barbecue grill will need to show that the handles do not tear under the stress of the weight when it is being carried by a person. In short, the government will get more involved with packaging, and organizations will have no choice other than to conform.

Environmental concerns

In the future, no industry will be able to escape the monitoring of environmental watchdogs. These scrutinizing groups are becoming stronger and more vocal, and they show no indication of backing down. Unfortunately, this will negatively impact the packaging industry since a major focus will be put on the recycling of packaging materials. Companies will need to invest time and effort into coming up with recyclable materials that meet the demands of environmentalists. This concern will present challenges, but it can be overcome....and the end result will be beneficial for consumers and organizations.

Cost factors

Future environmental concerns, technology, regulatory intervention, and consumer demands will combine to make packaging costs higher than they have ever been in the past. This cost cannot always be passed on to consumers, so other avenues will need to be explored to absorb it. One such avenue involves the condensing or concentration of products. Concentrated products require less packaging material, thereby lowering the unit cost. The consumer will still get the same amount of usages by simply using less of the product they purchase. An example includes concentrated laundry soap.

Another avenue involves lighter materials. At first glance, this might seem like it would do nothing, but it actually has three distinct benefits. First, it reduces the use of the materials. If a package is 20 percent lighter using the same material, then 20 percent less of that material is used thereby lowering the cost. Second, lighter packaging saves storage space. More packages can be warehoused in the same amount of warehouse space. Third, lighter packaging saves transportation costs. More units can be shipped for the same amount of money, thereby lowering the overall cost.

As you can see, packaging in the future will need to change to meet the demands of consumers, environmentalists, and business leaders. It will ultimately get better, but it will also face challenges that require change.

Regardless of the changes that are made to packages, the products they protect will need to be stored somewhere before they reach their final destination. This leads us to the next major focus of this book...commonly known as warehousing.

Warehousing

Introduction

Warehouses are areas where products are stored after they are packaged and before they are sold to customers. They are a necessary part of many businesses because those businesses need inventory to fill customer orders.

Warehouses are typically very structured. They have designated areas for every product so employees have an idea of where they need to go when they fill customer orders. For example, a furniture warehouse has bedroom furniture in one area and office furniture in another area. Additionally, most warehouses store the oldest products in the front to assure proper rotation. For example, a sausage manufacturer would have hot dogs with a sell-by date of February 17th in front of the hot dogs with a sell-by date of March 4th.

Products in inventory are often designated by stock-keeping units (also known as SKU). SKUs contain product numbers, product types, and product descriptions. This allows employees to search by barcode labels using scanning guns, which is much easier and faster than visually searching for products.

People manage warehouses in a variety of different ways. They often operate using methods that they are most comfortable with, but those methods are not necessarily the most efficient. The most efficient methods involve best practices....which are discussed in the next section.

Best practices

In terms of business, nothing is absolute. There are no perfect ways that assure success, and experimentation is often necessary to find out what works and what does not. Sometimes procedures used by other companies can be implemented and tweaked to fit the needs of a specific organization. That being said, some basic guidelines can be used as starting points for running a warehouse. These guidelines are also known as best practices, and they are listed below.

Set-up

Without proper setup, any best practices that follow will be hindered. Some aspects of this are simple such as making sure bays store products vertically rather than horizontally, keeping like products together, and providing room for jacks and Hi-Los to operate. However, other pieces of set-up puzzle require thorough analysis such as deciding which type of software to purchase, defining specific personnel responsibilities, and mapping out the entire process flow from receiving to shipping.

Regardless of the amount of time and effort put into the set-up, it must be done correctly for the smooth implementation of other best practices. This is essentially the planning phase of warehousing, and "those who fail to plan, plan to fail."

Receiving

Receiving marks the beginning of the warehouse process. It is where the product comes into the storage area for shipping at some point in the future (hopefully the near future). Once products enter the warehouse, they become the responsibility of warehouse personnel. Packaging employees have done their jobs, and products move to their final destination before they reach customers.

Documentation is necessary to show what products have been moved from the packaging department to the warehouse. A log should be maintained to show what has been received. This log is useful for warehouse personnel, but it can also be used by employees in other departments. Accountants, inventory control personnel, and salespeople all use this information to help them do their jobs better. Accountants assign different costs and values to finished products in storage, inventory control personnel move products from in-process to finished, and salespeople know they have finished products available to sell to customers.

Products that are wrongly packaged, labeled, or coded need to be stopped at receiving and sent back for corrective action. This action puts the responsibility back on the shoulders of packaging personnel and prevents customers from becoming upset about faulty products.

In short, receiving cannot be taken lightly because it is very important for organizations. It is the last internal check before products are transported, and it could prevent problems from occurring once those products are in the field.

Flow

This refers to the movement of products once they are in the warehouse. It requires employees who know how to drive powered jacks and forklifts and are certified for doing so. Most states offer powered industrial lift written tests that certify operators. Operators who answer questions incorrectly simply need to be shown the correct answers and sign off that they understand where their mistakes were made.

Unfortunately, understanding how to properly operate powered jacks and forklifts is a simple aspect of best practices for inventory flow. It is much more difficult to accurately pick orders for customers. Order picking involves finding the product, selecting the correct amount, and making sure the oldest product is selected first. A FIFO (first in, first out) system is helpful for properly selecting the rotating stock, but it does not guarantee success. Many problems in warehouses stem from orders that were not picked properly or stock that was not rotated. Erroneous order picking leads to inaccurate inventory numbers that negatively impact many people's jobs. Scanning guns and software programs make this process easier, but they are also not foolproof. In short, employees who pick orders need to be able to think and reason.

Shipping

After the product has been picked, it is moved to the shipping dock. It remains on the dock until it is loaded on a truck for transport to the customer or distributor. This might seem like a fairly cut-and-dry process, but some concerns require the implementation of best practices due to the potential for the following:

Theft

> Dishonest people are always looking for opportunities to steal, and shipping docks often provide those opportunities. Products that are temporarily stored on docks tend to go unwatched, and thieves take advantage of that lack of monitoring. They steal individual products...and they even take entire pallets of products if they are able to back their trucks into wells. Typically, products with high values are targeted by these criminals, but they will pilfer anything they can profit from.

Damage

> Damage can occur for a variety of different reasons. Some products become contaminated due to malicious individuals while other products are damaged due to the careless or accidental actions of employees. Examples include puncturing a hole in an oil barrel causing it to leak all over the dock, hitting a pallet of pens with the forklift of a Hilo causing the pens to break and fall out of their boxes, or leaving meat on a dock too long causing it to spoil. All of these examples can be caused by mistakes or purposeful intent...but the point is that they can and do occur.

Loading mistakes

> Product might make it all the way to the truck before a problem occurs. Examples include (1) loading the wrong amount of product on a truck and (2) putting the correct amount of product on the wrong truck. Typically, loading mistakes are accidental, but they are still a shipping concern.

Based on the potential for problems, it is rather obvious that products on shipping docks need to be watched closely. One way to do this is to have o have a shipping manager who monitors all shipping related activity. This individual spends most of his or her working day on the dock floor and has a "fishbowl" office with windows that allow unrestricted viewing of all dock happenings.

Another way to safeguard products on shipping docks is to restrict shipping dock access to authorized personnel. Locked doors with codes, keys, or swipe cards can be used to restrict personnel and prevent wrongful activities. Locks also limit the number of potentially responsible people when there is a problem that needs to be investigated...especially if time stamps and names are documented every time a person unlocks a door.

The third method of monitoring involves the use of cameras. Cameras are placed at strategic points so that every inch of the receiving dock is under surveillance 24/7. Cameras serve a dual purpose. First, and foremost, they monitor all activity which means anything anyone does is filmed. The second purpose of cameras involves deterrence. When people know their actions are being monitored, they are less likely to do something that they know is wrong. In terms of theft, cameras are well worth the investment.

Safety

Safety is a best practice of a warehouse that is often overlooked because it takes time and costs money. However, lack of safety can result in situations that require a lot of time and money. Rules should be in place to keep aisles clear, prevent riding on jacks and other horseplay, and make sure powered lift trucks are operating properly. These rules need to be enforced, and disciplinary action needs to be taken when they are broken.

You are now aware of some best practices that can be used to combat the challenges involved with managing a warehouse. Unfortunately, these challenges will never completely go away as long as people are part of the process. That being said, there is a need for warehouses to be better managed....and that is why improvement is the focus of the next section.

Improving

As astute leaders are well aware, there is room for improvement in virtually every aspect of organizations. The "if it ain't broke, don't fix it" mentality simply does not apply to businesses that strive for growth and prosperity. This means the management and operation of warehouses get better, and specific suggestions for improvement include:

80/20 rule

This is a rather old rule that still has value in modern warehouses. It saves order picking time by designating specific areas for higher volume products. In short, 20 percent of the warehouse holds items that constitute 80 percent of all customer orders. This means order pickers are not traveling all over the warehouse to get the majority of items they pick in a normal day.

The 80/20 rule does not work for every warehouse because they all do not have an 80/20 mix of product sales. However, it can improve many different types of warehouses because it saves time, thereby making those operations more efficient.

Fewer boxes

Less is often more...especially when it comes to boxes. This suggestion is beneficial for warehouses that use many different boxes when packaging their products. Packaging engineers can design boxes that house multiple products, thereby reducing the number of boxes that need to be inventoried and the different types of pallet configurations required for products. In short, fewer boxes improve warehouses by saving time, creating space, and simplifying processes.

Technology

Warehouses can get better by improving technology. This technology consists of software and systems as shown below:

Software

New software for computerized devices is always being created, and much of it does wonders for improving warehousing. For example, barcoding uses software for generating accurate and reliable information. This technology allows for the tracking of raw materials to determine where they came from, where they are, where they are going, and when they need to be re-ordered.

The advantages of barcoding are error reduction and time savings. Accuracy is not dependent on human entry, and information can be inputted in a fraction of the time required by manual methods.

Systems

Conveyor systems are a simple method for improving the efficiency of warehousing. Conveyors transfer product from one area to another with much less labor when compared to manual transfer by employees. In short, they facilitate warehouse processes and can be set up relatively inexpensively. Some conveyor systems do not even need motors, relying on gravity or spinning wheels for product transfer.

Incentives

Employee incentives are a much-debated way to improve warehouses. Some people argue that incentives provide employee motivation...but others argue that they create unnecessary employee competition. However, when utilized properly incentives can be beneficial. People want to be rewarded for their efforts, and incentives provide that reward. If they work harder, they earn more money...so many people choose to work harder. This creates a win-win situation because employees increase their wages and warehouses increase their efficiency.

As you can see, warehousing can be improved in several different ways. The last section of this book looks beyond improvement by exploring the future of warehouses.

Future

This section explores the future of warehousing. Most of the changes that take place will be financially driven, and they will require better management skills for the people in charge. These changes will include:

Less space

In terms of space, warehouses of the future will need to do more with less. This will require managers to think about processes and procedures before making decisions. High-performance equipment will need to be chosen, storage areas will need to be used wisely, waste will need to be reduced, and organizational efficiency will need to improve. That being said, managers of the future will be smarter and more adaptable than they are today. They will accept change on a moment's notice and be willing to venture into the unknown. They will enlarge their minds rather than their buildings to resolves space-related issues, and this will benefit their bottom lines.

Lower inventory

Similar to the future of warehouse space, inventories of the future will also be reduced. Inventoried product costs money to keep on hand, and that money is not recouped until that product is sold. This will require more preparation, better forecasting, and faster reaction time on the part of managers. Based on these changes, planning will become a very important aspect of warehouse managers' jobs….and that importance will continue to increase as time goes on.

Reduce product weight

Business leaders understand that increased product weight adds cost to the entire warehousing process. Because of this, engineers will work to reduce the weight of products stored in warehouses. This change will make employees' jobs easier and reduce their injuries while lowering transportation costs for the organization. It will result in happier workforces in warehouses and healthier bottom lines for organizations.

Better technology

Technology was mentioned earlier as a way to improve warehousing…and that technology will be available in the future. Warehouse managers will have access to software that simplifies their jobs and saves their organizations money. This software will also reduce employee stress and make their jobs easier. In short, it will benefit every employee involved with the warehousing aspects of organizations.

Radio Frequency Identification (RFID) is an example of better technology will be used more frequently in the future. Warehouses that move thousands of items through their faculties need inventorying systems that are more efficient than barcoding. For these companies, radio frequency identification (RFID) is the answer. Essentially, RFID uses radio waves to collect information on products and raw materials. That information gathered is similar to that collected by bar code scanners, but it can be read from several feet away. That being said, some readers are mounted on walls or ceilings as they accurately scan all items that pass by them.

The advantages of RFID are volume and readability. Large numbers of raw materials or finished products can be scanned without the necessity of hand-held units, and these scanners do not have to have a direct line of sight to register information. However, RFID has some technical issues and privacy concerns that need to be ironed out before it will be completely accepted.

In terms of RFID technology, there are no concrete regulations in effect, so one company's system might not be able to be read by another. This is especially troubling when the customers of manufacturers are unable to scan the items they are receiving. Additionally, these systems are difficult to program and there is a constant threat of information being intercepted. Based on these disadvantages, some warehouses are shying away from RFID...at least until the technology gets better and the risk for problems decreases.

Summary

This book focuses on packaging and warehousing in product-based organizations. The first section examines types, purposes, and advantages of packaging; while the last section explores best practices and improvement of warehousing. The future of both of these areas is also discussed. The text is informational and educational, and it is written for easy understanding at all reader levels.

Congratulations! You now understand more about packaging and warehousing...two important areas for many different types of organizations.

Distribution and Transportation

Management, Challenges, and Manufacturing Influences

Louis Bevoc

Published by
NutriNiche System LLC

For information contact:
info@nutriniche.com

Louis Bevoc books...simple explanations of complex subjects

Introduction

Manufacturers are often judged by their production capability. In other words, their worth to their customers and others they conduct business with is determined by the amount of product they can produce in a given amount of time. Typically, higher production numbers reduce the cost of manufacturing, and that cost reduction can be passed on to subsequent stops on the supply chain. Since price drives consumer demand for most products, cost reduction usually plays a major role in business transactions of manufacturers...especially if the products involved are commodity rather than specialty items.

Without a doubt, production capability is important for manufacturers, but it is not the only aspect of their businesses that affects the costs of the products they produce. Many other variables come into play, including distribution and transportation. Without distribution and transportation, products cannot be inventoried and shipped; thereby making production capacity completely irrelevant. In other words, regardless of how much product is produced, it has to reach customers to complete the sale...and this is done with distribution and transportation.

This book discusses the challenges faced by product distribution and transportation companies and the impact of manufacturing on these companies. Every organization faces challenges, but transportation and distributing companies face special challenges because (1) they do not have control over many aspects of their businesses, and (2) their value on the supply chain is always under scrutiny. Both of these challenges are examined in this book.

Before getting into the crux of this book, it is important to realize that distributing and transportation are not the same. They have some similarities, but they also have some differences. In fact, these differences are sometimes so great that companies choose to focus on the distribution aspect of the transportation aspect rather than both. In other words, they are a distribution company or a transportation company...not a distribution and a transportation company.

Please keep in mind that there are organizations that distribute products and transport them to customers, but they are beginning to become less common. Company leaders want their business models to be as simple as possible, and the combination of distribution and transportation adds complexity. These leaders also want their companies to be very good at what they do, and often times this is best achieved by doing one thing only.

Below are brief descriptions of product distribution and product transportation.

Distribution

Distribution is the process whereby manufacturers make their products available to end-users. This process can be handled directly by the manufacturer or it can be outsourced to secondary channels known as distributors. Distributors take physical possession of manufacturers' products, maintain an inventory, and move those products to designated destinations.

Some distribution companies have manufactures private label products for them so they can build their own brand with their distribution network. Other distributors contract transportation companies to move product for them rather than make transportation part of their operation. Hiring transportation companies might appear to defeat the purpose of a distribution company, but it makes sense if transportation companies can do the job more efficiently and cost-effectively.

Transportation

Similar to distribution, transportation is also a process that makes products available to end-users, but it focuses on the methods by which that product is physically moved or transferred. It is a part of the distribution process that can stand by itself or be part of a distributing company.

Unlike distributors, transportation companies rarely take physical possession of products or have manufacturers private label products for them. They specialize in moving other companies' products from point A to Point B in the most cost-effective and efficient way possible. In short, they specialize in transportation, and they focus all of their efforts on this specialization.

Now that you have a broad idea of what defines distribution and transportation, we can move into a more detailed discussion on how they operate, the challenges they encounter, and how they are influenced by manufacturing. Let's start with distribution.

Distribution

Distribution has a goal of ensuring products get to customers as quickly and efficiently as possible. In order to accomplish this task, it requires solid warehousing and transportation. Warehousing involves inventorying manufacturers' products and transportation involves moving those products. As mentioned earlier, transportation can be a separate function performed by another company or it can be part of the distribution company.

For the most part, distributors operate under three basic management systems that determine when and what products need to be purchased and who is responsible for overseeing the internal processes. These three management systems seek similar goals of customer satisfaction and cost efficiency, but they operate quite differently.

The first management system, known as system 1, is controlled by manufacturers before their products reach the distributor's door. In system 1, manufacturers understand the needs of the end-user and replenish stock based on that knowledge. Needs are forecasted and products are made as required. This system is great when forecasting is accurate because it allows for seamless production and flows through the distribution phase without product shortages or overages. However, inaccurate forecasts can disrupt the flow of product and cause major shortages or overages. Essentially, the entire system is built upon the manufacturer's understanding of end-user needs.

An example of system 1 management involves Bretterin Tool. Bretterin manufactures tools for a chain of hardware stores. They have made tools for these hardware stores for over 20 years, and they have access to data regarding each individual store's needs. They have no problem producing the products needed, but they are not set up to deliver to the individual stores located in Michigan, Ohio, and Illinois. They contract a Queenie Distribution to deliver to the individual stores, but that is the extent of Queenie's role. Tools are shipped product based on forecasts made by the manufacturer, and Queenie relies on those forecasts to avoid shortages or overages. In short, stock replenishment is manufacturer driven.

The second management system, known as system 2, is controlled by managers at the distribution company. In system 2, distributors understand the needs of the end-user and replenish stock based on that knowledge. They forecast the needs of end-users and order from manufacturers as required. This system is great when forecasting is accurate because it allows distributors to have a "finger on the pulse" of their customers. However, inaccurate forecasts can disrupt the flow of product and upset manufacturers and customers; thereby resulting in the distribution company shouldering the entire blame. Essentially, this system is built upon the distributor's understanding of the end user's needs.

An example of system 2 management involves Kittles Distribution. Kittles buys several different types of dolls from Spencer Manufacturing, a toy manufacturer. Kittles sells many independent toy stores in the metro Chicago area, and orders from these stores do not adhere to specific patterns. Kittles' salespeople are in the stores, and they provide orders for managers at the distribution company who decide what and when dolls stock needs to be replenished. In short, stock replenishment is distributor driven.

The third management system, known as system 3, is controlled by the end-user or customer. In system 3, end-users understand their own needs and replenish stock based on that knowledge. They forecast their needs and contact their distributors who then order from manufacturers. This is probably the most accurate management system because end users are responsible for making sure they get what they need. However, those end users are stuck with the problems they create and, if severe enough, those problems can put them out of business. If they go out of business, the distributors and manufacturers are also negatively affected.

An example of system 3 management involves Yendis Distributors. Yendis is the distribution division of a corporation that owns 200 sub shops in California and Nevada. These stores follow a strict operation protocol determined by the corporate office and they are not allowed to deviate. For example, if one type of sub is put on sale, then every store has to put that sub on sale for the same price. This rigid structure allows store managers to know what they are going to sell every day. Based on this knowledge, the store managers call in their orders to the distributor every Thursday by noon, and distributors purchase food and suppliers from manufacturers based on those orders. In short, stock replenishment is end user-driven.

Now, let's explore some of the hurdles that distributing companies must overcome to be successful. These hurdles are known as distribution challenges, and they are discussed below.

Inventory management

Inventory is a challenge for any company that takes physical possession of products because those products cost money. Money is necessary for the purchasing of the products, the space they occupy, and the time necessary for managing the inventory process. If the money spent becomes excessive, then companies start to see it in their bottom lines as their profits erode.

Distributors are impacted by inventory more than just about any other type of business. In fact, inventory management is the key to a distributor's success or failure. Manager's need to assure that the necessary inventory is on hand to fill their customers' orders without having too much stock and running the risk of their products becoming liabilities instead of assets. To do this, they need to understand supply and demand, forecasting, and finance, as well as having the ability to react to change. This understanding and ability are optimal when managers have full visibility of their workplaces.

Full visibility of the distribution workplace cannot be achieved without real-time data. Real-time inventory data is information that becomes available as soon as a product enters or exits stock. It allows managers to view purchase orders for products that are going to be kept in stock and sales order for items that are going to leave stock. It also shows inventory movement during all stages of the distribution process, from receiving to delivery at the customer's doorstep. This is not a simple task; thereby making it challenging for distributors, but it has been made easier with technology specifically geared toward inventory management.

The main technology used for inventory management is known as Radio Frequency Identification (RFID). In a nutshell, RFID tracks inventory from start to finish using electromagnetic fields that track products and identify their whereabouts at all times. Tracking usually begins when a product enters the distributing company's facility and ends when the product exits the facility. However, more complex systems start the tracking immediately after a product is manufactured and continues until the product hits the end user's doorstep.

Regardless of the technology available, inventory management is a challenge for distributors of all products. Generally speaking, bigger inventories equate to bigger headaches due to the amount of product and information that needs to be tracked and stored.

Management systems

As mentioned earlier in this book, three basic management systems dictate the way distributors operate. These systems all have advantages and disadvantages, but how do distribution leaders know which system is best for their company? This is often a difficult question to answer because it requires understanding where the business is now and where it will be in the future.

Most distribution leaders have an understanding of where their company is now, but predicting where it will be in the future is a challenging task...and inaccurate predictions can cause problems that require time and money to resolve. In severe cases, these problems cannot be resolved and the affected distributors are forced to shut their doors.

Unfortunately, there is no easy way to rise above the challenge of selecting the correct management system. It takes input from the manufacturing, distribution, and customer areas of the chain to decide the direction that needs to be taken. If the customers know exactly what they want, then they should make decisions about product replenishment. If manufacturers understand the needs of their customers based on experience, then they should replenish inventory as they see fit. If distributors have a "finger on the pulse" of their customers, then they should make product replenishment decisions. However, regardless of the management direction taken, distributors need to communicate internally and externally before making decisions.

Middleman status

Many people are familiar with the phrase, "eliminate the middleman." This is based on the thinking that there is no need for someone in the middle to get involved. All that involvement does is increase cost, add a step to the process, and create more paperwork.

Manufacturers have the ability to eliminate the middleman by making the distribution part of their operation. However, this course of action requires a lot of resources that are not normally part of the production process, and it adds a huge burden. It is not that manufacturers cannot distribute, it is simply that distribution is not what they do best. They specialize in manufacturing, and they will be most successful by focusing on that specialization. However, the fact that they can form a distributorship at any time puts pressure on distributors to perform optimally...and optimal performance day-after-day is challenging for any business.

Distributors will always be the middleman in business because they purchase products from manufacturers and sell them to end-users. If they do their jobs effectively, then they typically do not have to worry about being eliminated because manufacturers do not want the headaches that go along with distribution....they gladly hand those headaches off to the next phase of the supply chain.

In short, elimination of the middleman might be good in some business situations, but it is not always the answer for distribution decisions. Unfortunately, it is a battle that distributors need to win to stay in business.

Customer expectations

Customers have always had demands in terms of expectations, but these demands have increased in recent years due to the continuous, and seemingly endless, technological advances. While it is true that technology has made many aspects of business easier and faster for distribution companies, it has not increased the speed that truck can drive from one point to another. Unfortunately, many customers expect the speed of delivery to increase, and they are disappointed when it does not. Add this to the fact that Amazon.com delivers just about anything in two days or less, and it is understandable why many distributors cannot meet their customers' expectations.

The above paragraph paints a rather bleak picture for distribution companies in terms of customer expectations, but, in reality, it is not all bad. Distributors that are able to keep products in stock, ship full orders, and meet agreed-upon delivery dates will always have value for end-users. That value might not be quite what it once was in the past, but it is still there and customers realize its importance.

Now that you understand the basics of distribution, let's move on to the next step of the process known as transportation.

Transportation

Transportation is the physical process of moving products from one point to another. Transportation can be part of a manufacturing company, part of a distribution company, or a completely separate company that functions independently. However, regardless of its status as a business, transportation has a goal of physically moving products in the most efficient and cost-effective manner.

Most people think of product transportation occurring in large trucks towing filled semi-trailers. They picture big cabs where drivers can sleep instead of paying for motels, and they visualize these drivers going to the various truck stops found along major highways and eating, refueling, relaxing, or using the restroom facilities. This thinking does apply to many long-haul truck drivers who spend weeks or even months on the road, but they are by no means the only method of transportation. In addition to trucking over roads, transportation also takes place via water, rail, air, and pipelines. The following describes the major types of transportation:

Road

Transportation of product that takes place over roads can involve many types of vehicles. For example, a farmer might use a tractor to transport corn to a mill located a few miles away or a motorcycle might be used by a restaurant employee to deliver a pizza. However, most road transportation takes place using trucks.

Truck transportation usually involves moving trailered products across roads for delivery. Most products are in bins or on pallets so they can be loaded and unloaded with forklifts or pallet jacks, but other products, such as machines with wheels, might simply be placed on the trailer floor.

The advantages and disadvantages of road transportation are as follows:

Advantages

Service - This is likely the biggest advantage because road vehicles can deliver products directly to customers' doorsteps. The products do not have to be dropped off at an airport, station, or port and then moved to the end-user. Additionally, products can reach customers in rural areas that might not be accessible by plane, train, or boat.

Damage risk - Road vehicles are the best way to ship delicate items that are at risk of being damaged or broken. This is because products are not stacked on top of each other like they are in planes, trains, and boats due to the need for large amounts of cargo in limited space. Additionally, barring accidents, products shipped in road vehicles are less likely to be damaged by sudden movements that occur during elevated speeds or violent movements. Planes and trains often travel hundreds of miles per hour, and ships usually face rough waters at some time during the voyage.

Disadvantages

Traffic - Traffic can cause major issues for products transported over the road. In fact, traffic problems can bring vehicles to a complete stand-still; thereby creating situations where product cannot be delivered on time. If traffic issues become too much of a problem, then customers will look for other methods of product delivery.

Climate – Weather has a big impact on road transportation. Wet or slippery conditions force drivers to slow down; thereby delaying delivery of the products they are moving. However, poor weather also leads to accidents that can delay or prevent drivers from reaching their destinations.

Biggest challenge

Transportation of products by road can be challenging as indicated by the disadvantages above, but one challenge that stands out above the rest is driver shortages. Without drivers, products do not get shipped and customers are not happy. However, regardless of the amount of advertising and recruiting that takes place, the demand for truck drivers always seems to exceed the supply.

Water

Transportation of products that takes place over water typically involves a boat or ship. These two vessels are essentially the same, but a ship is bigger than a boat and it is often designed to carry cargo while boats are designed to carry people.

Water transportation takes place on rivers, canals, lakes, and oceans. Smaller bodies of water such as ponds might also be used for moving products, but this type of transportation is rare. Large freighters are often used on oceans to move products internationally, but large lakes, such as the great lakes, can also be navigated by freighters. Typically, smaller boats and ships carry products on rivers, canals, and small lakes.

The advantages and disadvantages of water transportation are as follows:

Advantages

Cost – Water is usually the cheapest way to transport products because it typically does not require construction or maintenance. The exception to this is canals which are dug and maintained, but canals are also used for other purposes such as irrigation or removing water from otherwise bogged land.

Capacity – Water transport vessels can carry a lot of cargo....much more than a truck or plane. Some products, such as wood (timber), use water as their main source of movement due to the size and weight involved. In short, large or bulky items find water transportation very valuable.

Disadvantages

Water conditions – Water conditions can create very difficult situations for ships. For example, frozen water cannot be navigated without special equipment, and rough water can damage cargo. Add to this the fact that weather can be unpredictable, and it is easy to understand why water conditions are a disadvantage for the transportation of products.

Limited application – As noted earlier, ships can carry a lot of freight. In fact, large volume is typically "the name of the game" for water transportation. Small businesses typically do not need a lot of volume shipped, so they cannot use water transportation to their advantage. Additionally, shipping vessels usually stack products on top of each other, and this is not good for items that damage easily.

Biggest challenge

Lack of control is likely the biggest challenge for the transportation of products by water. Uncontrollable factors such as temperature, ice blockages, high winds, and rough waters can damage cargo and delay deliveries. More importantly, severe weather conditions create unsafe conditions for crew members, and people who are not careful can be injured or lose their lives.

Rail

Rail transportation is the movement of product from one point to another via trains. Trains are guided by the tracks that they run on. These tracks lead to designated areas all over the world, and they are known to go into places that are difficult to reach using water or road transportation.

Train engines (also known as locomotives) are capable of pulling many cars, from one to hundreds, so they can move quite a bit of cargo if necessary. This is possible due to the low friction they encounter on railroad tracks. That low friction also makes the movement of product on trains more energy efficient than other types of transportation.

The advantages and disadvantages of rail transportation are as follows:

Advantages

Safety- Trains do not fight much traffic, and their stops are determined before they start to move. They typically do not have to worry about sinking, losing altitude, or crashing into another train; thereby making them safer than water, air, and road transportation.

Climate - Rail transportation is less affected by weather than air, water, or road transportation. Rain, fog, heat, cold, snow, slush, and wind have little impact on the movement of a train. Earthquakes and tornados can stop a train in its tracks, but these types of disasters are rare; thereby making rail transportation a good choice when the climate is adverse.

Disadvantages

Speed - Trains are not the fasted way to transport products. They do not normally take shortcuts, nor do they have guaranteed overnight delivery services. If a product needs to be at a designated destination by 10:00 am the next morning, then rail is not the best method of transportation available.

Access - Access to rail networks is an issue for many businesses because trains do not go everywhere. If trains are not available, then other methods of transportation need to be used to move products from one destination to another.

Biggest challenge

Rail transportation has always lacked the ability to service people everywhere. Quite simply, road and air transportation are continually expanding; thereby offering access to more businesses while providing faster, more efficient, and more effective services for the movement of products. Unfortunately, lack of access was a problem for train transportation in the past, it is a problem today, and it will likely be a problem in the future.

Air

Many people do not realize the fact that air transportation is quite common simply because they do not see airplanes pulling up to their dock doors to deliver products. They see a truck, so they assume the product they have ordered was delivered in a truck. This assumption is partially true because a truck did take the product to the final destination. However, it might have been delivered to the truck via air transportation in order to speed up the process and provide more effective service.

Regardless of what people know or do not know about air transportation of products, it takes place all over the world. Planes carry cargo at all hours of the day to populated and unpopulated areas. In fact, a plane that delivers product to crowded areas of California might deliver those same products to desolate areas of Alaska.

The advantages and disadvantages of air transportation are as follows:

Advantages

Speed – Air transportation is by far the fastest way to move products because speeds reach hundreds of miles per hour, while other forms of transportation usually travel under 80 miles per hour. Add to this the fact that planes can fly a straight line without traffic interruptions, and it is easy to see why air travel is in a league of its own in terms of speed.

Lack of barriers – This refers to the lack of physical barriers due to the routes being free of water, trees, hills, mountains, valleys, and some types of weather issues such as slush and ice. Add to this the fact that there is no traffic to avoid, and it can easily be seen why lack of barriers is an advantage for air transportation.

Disadvantages

Fuel – The cost of fueling a plane can be very expensive, especially if heavy products are being transported. This cost can be too high for some businesses to absorb, regardless of their needs, so they choose to use other methods of transportation. This makes fuel a big disadvantage for the movement of product via airplanes.

Government intervention – Air travel has a wealth of regulations....and most of these regulations are for good reasons. Safety, security, and illegal activities need to be addressed before planes leave the ground to avoid in-air catastrophes. In terms of air transportation, it is better to be safe than sorry...but the protocols involved can be expensive and delay flights.

Biggest challenge

Congestion is the biggest challenge facing air transportation because the number and frequency of flights are continually increasing. Although this does not necessarily prevent products from reaching designated destinations, it can cause delays...and those delays are probably going to increase in the future. This means air transportation will be threatened with losing its grip on the fastest form or product transportation available.

Pipeline

This is likely the most unique and inexpensive type of transportation because products are loaded and unloaded with the opening of a valve, flick of a switch, or click of a mouse and most of the cost is upfront when building the pipelines.

Most people associated oil or water with pipeline transportation, but other products, such as kerosene and propylene, also use this movement method. In fact, most gases and liquids can use pipelines for transportation.

The advantages and disadvantages of pipeline transportation are as follows:

> **Reliability** – Pipelines are reliable product movement systems because they are relatively free of obstructions. Traffic and weather have little effect; thereby creating a continuous flow of product that cannot be achieved via any other method of transportation.

> **Space** – Pipelines can be run underground (or underwater); thereby having a limited impact on the environment above. In many cases, people go about their daily personal or work lives as products pass by under their feet. If they are not told that the pipeline is beneath the soil, they usually do not even know it exists.

Disadvantages

> **Diversity** – The biggest disadvantage of pipelines is the limited products that can utilize this method of transportation. Product must be some form of liquid, semi-liquid, soft solid, electricity, or gas to flow freely from one point to another. In other words, it is safe to say that appliances will never be transported via pipelines...unless technology changes drastically!

> **Leaks and pilferage** – Breaks in pipelines, regardless of whether they are accidental or purposeful, create many different problems. Purposeful breaks occur from illegal activities where the perpetrators steal the product being transported for their own economic gain. These breaks cost a lot of money due to the product that is stolen. However, accidental breaks are often even more expensive due to the lost product, environmental damage, and cost of cleanup.

Biggest challenge

Policing is probably the biggest challenge for pipeline transportation. It is difficult, if not impossible, to monitor every inch of the pipeline for damage or illegal activity. Some pipelines run for thousands of miles, so, understandably, they cannot be one hundred percent policed. Technology has made it easier for pipeline companies to monitor their business activities, but the system is far from perfect.

Summary

Distribution and transportation of products complete the process that starts at manufacturing and finishes at the end-user. Without distribution and transportation, manufacturers would be forced to inventory stock and deliver that stock to individual customers. This process requires a lot of resources that are not readily available to manufactures, and it is outside of most manufacturers' areas of expertise.

This book focuses on product distribution and transportation challenges and manufacturing Influences. The distribution section explores inventory, management systems, business status, and customer expectations. The transportation section discusses the major types including road, water, rail, air, and pipeline in addition to highlighting the advantages and disadvantages of each type. The text is informational and educational and it is written at a level that is easily understandable at all reader levels.

Congratulations! You now understand more about the challenges of and manufacturing influences on distribution and transportation......aspects of business responsible for moving products from one point to another.

Blockchain
in Manufacturing

Explaining the Basics

Louis Bevoc and Allison Shearsett

Published by
NutriNiche System LLC

For information contact:
info@nutriniche.com

Louis Bevoc books...simple explanations of complex subjects

Introduction

Blockchain technology has grown to the point where it is now trendy to talk about it in manufacturing businesses around the world. This interest has transpired because blockchain provides complete traceability for products. Essentially, it puts a permanent time stamp on every stop (aka block) during the assembly of a product and then follows that product through to the retail shelf. In short, everything in the supply chain is documented so, if there is a problem, that problem can be traced to the source for resolution.

In a nutshell, blockchain is a record-keeping system where each record is referred to as a block. These blocks are linked using a secure system that stores information and makes it accessible at any time for anyone on the network. Each block has a permanent timestamp that cannot be changed. Notes can be added that refer back to something that underwent a change, but the stamp can never be altered.

The concept of blockchain has been around for almost three decades. The thinking behind it back then revolved around the development of a chain of secure documents that could not be tampered with by anyone. Eventually, this early version incorporated "blocks" where data could be stored and transferred intact to other blocks. This incorporation allowed for the transfer of large secured blocks of information that prevented others from making up information that best suited their needs.

Blockchain continued to progress over time, but it had a limited following until the advent of bitcoin. Bitcoin needed a way to log and total all of its economic transactions, and blockchain was chosen to get the job done. In this capacity, blockchain served as a public ledger for all dealings on the bitcoin network. The subsequent explosion in popularity of bitcoin thrust blockchain into the spotlight and led to it becoming the traceability choice for a variety of manufacturers around the globe.

After bitcoin opened the door, other organizations started to look at blockchain as a security system. However, while this technology is a popular conversation piece among chief information officers in many corporations, it has yet to gain a strong foothold in terms of actual usage. In short, blockchain has generated a lot of interest, but most companies have not taken it past the discussion stage.

The above introduction falls well short of describing the complete history of blockchain because many people have spent countless hours working on and improving this technology. It has come a long way since its inception and it will be adopted by more and more manufacturers...especially those that use multiple components in the assembly of their products. However, this introduction does provide a brief idea of the thinking behind blockchain, and it helps lead us into the next section that provides a more detailed analysis of this record-keeping system.

What is blockchain?

A full-blown discussion on blockchain requires much more detail than is found within the pages of this book, but the intent of this book is not to provide a detailed analysis. Instead, it is designed to explain the basics concept of this technology in terms of manufacturing so it can be easily understood by the average person.

Blockchain has been described by some people as a new type of internet. While this might or might not be true, it can be said with confidence that it has made changes to the internet because it allows the transfer of information that cannot be copied or changed; thereby making it valuable for business leaders who want factual traceability without the threat of it being stolen, altered, or misused.

The best way to visualize blockchain is to picture a spreadsheet that is shared with hundreds, thousands, or millions of people on a network. Every time a change is made to that spreadsheet, it is immediately viewed by everyone on the network; thereby allowing information to be shared instantaneously. Other networks allow the instantaneous sharing of information, but blockchain is unique because information is not stored in a centralized location.

Decentralization is the first important aspect that defines blockchain. Blockchain networks are decentralized rather than centralized, and this decentralization offers two distinct advantages. First, the information is available simultaneously to anyone on the network. It is not controlled by a single person or group of people who choose the information that is made available for viewing. Second, decentralized networks prevent hacking because the information is not stored in a single location. This adds great value because files cannot be hacked or corrupted.

The second important aspect that defines blockchain is its permanence. Once a block is created, it cannot be deleted or changed. This has great importance for fact-gathering when looking back on a process or procedure because there is no altering of what transpired. Unfortunately, it is not uncommon for people to change documentation so it is advantageous for their own purposes...but blockchain prevents this from occurring.

The third defining aspect of blockchain is the fact that it is digital. Information from the system is never printed on paper; thereby saving time, space, and resources. The digital format also makes sense because, as more and more people log information on the network, changes become continuous, and maintaining them in paper form would require an endless amount of time and money. Without a doubt, digital storage and sharing of information have big advantages over paper storage and sharing in terms of resource usage.

The fourth, and final, important defining aspect of blockchain is it functions as a ledger that provides a simple way to verify transactions are real and accurate. It does this by recording the sequence of transactions in chronological order; thereby making all information transparent. In short, ledgers provide time-stamped documents that prevent fraudulent activity from all parties involved.

Uses

Now that you have a basic idea of the history and concept of blockchain, it is time to discuss some of its uses. Below are some areas where this technology has been found to be beneficial. Please keep in mind that these are just a few of the uses that currently exist, and readers who desire additional information should seek resources with more detailed explanations of the blockchain application.

Data storage

Many software systems store data, but blockchain stands out from the majority of them because it has a decentralized network. When data is stored, it remains stored and is never lost. Add this to the fact that the data cannot be changed or deleted, and it is easy to see why blockchain is a wise choice for many organizations.

Regulations

Many transactions, especially those that are legal or financial, are regulated by the government or other authorities. Blockchain provides transparency that is rivaled by few other systems and, when combined with the truthfulness of information, it makes an excellent choice for managing transactions with regulatory or other external party requirements.

In terms of regulations, blockchain has an added dimension of use because it can prevent people from being accused of or being found guilty of illegal activities. These illegal activities might have been conducted knowingly or unknowingly, but, either way, the end result could be prison time for those who do not follow regulatory requirements.

Data management

Blockchain allows users to manage their data for several reasons including (1) privacy of certain information and (2) selling information when it generates desired internet activity. This technology is so advanced that it can split data into fractional amounts for distribution to specified parties. Does this sound confusing to you? If so, then you are not alone because these types of activities are only fully understood by a select few people. However, the point is that blockchain is an excellent way to manage data by only exposing selected information and allowing users to benefit from that exposure.

Contracts

This refers to contracts that need to be "smart" to execute when conditions arrive or specifications are met. For example, a payout might need to be made when a company's stock reaches a certain value…and blockchain technology makes sure that payout is accurately made. This opens the door for direct interactions between specified parties without fear of mistakes or unscrupulous activity.

In a sense, blockchain acts as an overseer that might have required humans in the past. It can be programmed to factor many different variables into the equation including legal ramifications, verification of identities, registration requirements, and protection of intellectual property. Contracts that are complex, detailed, binding, and irreversible need blockchain technology to assure they are fulfilled as expected.

Audits

This refers to the auditing of people and processes to verify the entered information is accurate and the results are meeting specified standards. Audits are typically conducted by third parties who might or might not be affiliated with the organizations being audited. However, regardless of the connection, audits are designed to assure compliance with designated specifications, and accuracy and truthfulness are strongpoints of blockchain technology.

Blockchain has the ability to make everyone accountable for their actions. It can eliminate errors and stop the missed transactions that bog down many organizations. However, the goal of this book is to provide an understanding of blockchain in manufacturing, and that understanding starts with the next section.

Manufacturing

Blockchain is designed to follow a manufactured product from start to finish without missing any steps in-between. For example, a company that manufactures tires starts documenting at the rubber trees and finishes at the time of purchase by the end-user (customer). This is important because the stores that sell the tires usually do not have traceability at the time of sale. If customers complain about the tires, then a store only knows that they bought the tires from a distributor that dealt directly with the manufacturer. Therefore, the manufacturer needs to be able to trace their raw materials and know who purchased their finished products.

Traceability is especially important for safety concerns. Using the tire example above, a side blowout might require the manufacturer to know the source of tire belts in order to fix the problem. There is not a lot of time because the tire store is under pressure for answers, and it might possibly be facing a lawsuit. An error might have been made when the manufacturer's supplier produced the belts or the problem could have stemmed from the supplier's source of raw materials. Regardless of where the problem took place, accurate information is needed to trace the source and that accuracy can be obtained using blockchain technology. With blockchain, the manufacturer is assured that nothing is made up or altered so any information collected is real.

It can be argued that the supplier is responsible for all transactions that take place prior to them producing the belts and selling them to the manufacturer. However, there is no guarantee that they will have this information and, if they do have it, it might not be accurate or complete. Blockchain assures truthfulness and increases the probability of finding the problem and correcting it so it does not happen again.

Blockchain is important for manufacturers because it excels at finding problems in the supply chain. These problems typically allow for the pinpointing of mistakes that other companies have made; thereby allowing corrective action and preventative measures to be taken. However, blockchain technology also supplies information for manufacturers to see how they are performing internally. This type of information is great if management is willing to take action based on it...but, unfortunately, that is not always the case. Some managers have "tunnel vision" or do not want to spend the time and resources necessary for resolving their internal issues. They know they might have to move backward before moving forward, and they are not willing to move in a negative direction.

Food manufacturing

Blockchain is beneficial for all manufacturers, but it is particularly useful for food manufacturers due to the wide variety of ingredients that they put in their products and the fact that people who consume those products can become ill or die from foodborne illness. The following are examples of blockchain being used for food safety and food fraud.

Food safety

Food safety involves making sure food is safe when it reaches consumers. Many checks are in place during food processing to assure wholesome products, but sometimes those checks are not enough to prevent unsafe food from entering commerce. An example of a food safety issue that was resolved using blockchain involves a salad processor and foodborne illness.

Parnello Salad is a food processor that manufactures many different types of salads for food retail and foodservice operations. They purchase salad ingredients including various types of fruits, vegetables, nuts, meat, and cheese. They use blockchain technology for traceability and can pinpoint virtually every transaction on the supply chain.

In the middle of the summer, which is their busiest season, Parnello received a phone call from the buyer at one of their distributors. The buyer indicated she received complaints from four different stores that had customers become ill after eating Parnello salads. She demanded answers from Parnello management so she could tell her customers what happened.

After using blockchain to examine shipping documentation, Parnello's food safety manager determined that three different salads were involved in this crisis. All three salads had two common ingredients....iceberg lettuce and Swiss cheese. However, other salads with the same lettuce were not making customers ill, so it was determined that the cause of the illness was the Swiss cheese. The cheese was tested for pathogens at Parnello's microbiology lab and it was found to contain Listeria monocytogenes.

The CEO at Parnello immediately ordered a recall for all products containing the affected cheese. Blockchain provided the information based on ingredient logs kept for all products manufactured at the facility, and shipping logs showed who bought those products. In total, the recall affected over 100,000 pounds of salad.

Once the recall was in place, the root cause of the problem needed to be found. Blockchain was used to determine that the Swiss cheese was purchased from two different suppliers known as Wingleman's Dairy and Jupiter Foods. However, based on the coding system on all products, blockchain showed that the contaminated salads only contained cheese from Jupiter Foods. This was good information, but Jupiter Foods buys cheese from two different manufacturers, Hartville Milk Products and Valerie's Cheese Processing. Blockchain was used to trace the cheese used in the contaminated salads back to Valerie's Cheese Processing.

Parnello was now certain that the problem occurred at Valerie's Cheese Processing, and blockchain showed that the lot number of the contaminated cheese used in the affected salads was 2121A. This information was given to food safety personnel at Valerie's Cheese Processing, and they began an internal investigation. After examining records, it was found that lot 2121A did not reach proper cooking temperature due to a steam leak, but production personnel decided to use it anyway because they needed it to fill orders.

Blockchain showed that the steam leak had been repaired, but some type of measure had to be put in place to prevent a reoccurrence of the root problem (poor decision making). This measure consisted of food safety training for all employees to prepare them for future food safety decisions.

In the above example, the food safety crisis experienced by Parnello Salads could have been avoided if decisions were made with food safety in mind. However, this was not the case and order filling was the overriding factor. The end result was foodborne illness and a costly recall, but the problem had little chance of being discovered without blockchain technology.

Food fraud

In food manufacturing, food fraud is the economically motivated adulteration of products or processes. It is similar to food defense, but it focuses on economic rather than chemical, microbiological, and physical adulteration. An example of a food fraud issue that was resolved using blockchain involves the United States Department of Natural Resources' investigation of a fish company.

An experienced Department of Natural Resources (DNR) officer noticed local fish markets selling a wealth of tuna to customers. Upon inquiry, the officer found that all of these markets bought their fish from Bluefin Foods, a large tuna processor with over 1500 employees. She went to Bluefin Foods and asked them for their production volume of tuna for the past three months. Bluefin has a blockchain system in place which showed the officer that they produced 1,600,000 pounds. Blockchain also showed that the tuna was bought from two different commercial fishing companies known as Beckman Fishing and Russell Harvest.

Blockchain exposed the fact that Bluefin Foods purchased 1,100,000 pounds of tuna from Beckman Fishing and 500,000 pounds of tuna from Russell Harvest. This immediately threw up a red flag for the DNR office because she knew that the catch limit for Tuna is 800,000 pounds, yet Beckman Fishing sold 300,000 pounds more than that limit. Blockchain showed that Russell Harvest reported only catching 800,000 pounds of tuna, and the DNR Officer realized that this reported number was fraudulent.

The DNR officer met with Russell Harvest's owner, Captain Squayles, and he stated that his people must have improperly weighed the product. The DNR officer wrote a report, and DNR officials ruled that fraudulent activity had taken place. The DNR fined Russell Harvest $25,000 and placed them on probationary status for the next two tuna seasons.

In the above example, food fraud took place, and disciplinary action needed to be taken by a regulatory agency. This issue was discovered because blockchain technology indicated there was a discrepancy with time-stamped information based on government rules that were in place to protect over-fishing.

Unfortunately, things do not always work out as well as in the tuna example because, many times, nothing is in place to prevent a company from making up information or documenting actions that did not transpire. If wrongful entry of data occurs, then "garbage in equals garbage out" results and truthful information will not be yielded. For example, if a perfume manufacturer buys coloring ingredients from supplier A and lists supplier B as the source, then complete traceability means nothing...and it can lead to even more problems.

In manufacturing, "one up, one down" traceability refers to having documentation for first-tier suppliers of raw materials and first-tier customers purchasing finished products. However, a manufacturer's supply chain often involves many other parties that play an important role in the production process. The food safety and food fraud examples clearly indicate that blockchain is much more than a "one up, one down" traceability system because the problems were only identified after going further down the supply chain. For example, Parnello Salads would not have found the root cause of the foodborne illness if they stopped their investigation at their two Swiss cheese suppliers (Wingleman's Dairy and Jupiter Foods). Similarly, the DNR needed would not have imposed the fine and probationary period on Beckman Fishing if they stopped their investigation at Bluefin Foods.

As might be expected, there is a lot of debate over the usefulness of blockchain. Some people argue that it is not worth the difficulty of entering data, managing information, and navigating the system. Others argue that, without it, there are no guaranteed facts because information can always be changed or deleted. This book takes the stance that each manufacturer needs to decide on the worth of blockchain-based on the available information, and that is why the next section discusses the specific pros and cons of this technology.

Pros and cons

As might be expected, blockchain is not "the land of milk and honey." In fact, there are negatives associated with it that keep some manufacturers from using it as their traceability system. Essentially, management of each company to decide if blockchain is worthwhile by factoring in the advantages and disadvantages listed below. Please note that some of the pros and cons have already been discussed in this book while others were added for further clarity. However, the goal is to give readers a more concrete understanding of the blockchain system.

Advantages

- *External evaluation* – This is likely the biggest advantage for manufacturers using blockchain technology. They are able to evaluate every transaction within the supply chain from start to finish. When there is a problem, they are able to trace it to the original source and that source is a starting point for implementing measures that prevent it from happening again. In food manufacturing, this traceability process is referred to as "farm to fork" because it starts at the inception of raw materials and ends with the finished product being eaten by consumers.

- *Internal evaluation* - Every organization can improve in some way if managers within those organizations take the time to examine their internal shortcomings. Blockchain brings internal problems to the forefront by exposing them to everyone on the network. This is good because it makes the need for change obvious and prevents the tunnel vision that many managers have when it comes to areas where they need to improve. In this sense, blockchain functions as a tool that removes people from their comfort zones and makes them think about growing their organizations rather than sitting on the sidelines as opportunities pass by.

- *Security* – In terms of security, blockchain is an excellent choice for manufacturers. It has a decentralized network that cannot be high-jacked, dismantled, or destroyed. This anti-hacking capability assures the continuous flow of accurate information that allows anyone on the network to get what they need when they need it. Security is essential for any type of traceability system, and blockchain technology is more secure than any of its competitors.

Disadvantages

- *Lack of understanding* - Blockchain is about managing data, and it needs the involvement of every department in a manufacturing company. Production, quality, sales, marketing, shipping, receiving, accounting, and other departments need to be part of the process for it to work as designed. If a piece of the puzzle is missing, then the input of data will not be accurate and the end result will not reflect the truth of what transpired. Unfortunately, some managers falsely believe that blockchain is strictly a quality-driven function. They associate traceability problems with quality and throw it into the lap of the quality department along with "get it done" instructions. Quite simply, this does not work because input is needed from every department. If the quality department is responsible for the entire blockchain system, then that system will fail...and management will believe that they spent money for nothing in return.

- *Data security* - One might question why data security is a disadvantage of blockchain technology. After all, a major advantage of this technology is the decentralized networks that prevent hacking. However, the problem with security is that data can be seen by anyone on the network. This is very concerning for public networks, and that is why many organizations choose to keep their networks private. So, in a nutshell, people with access to the network cannot alter or delete data, but they can use it for wrongful reasons such as giving it to unauthorized individuals.

- *Resources* – As many people have experienced, it takes time and money to create work-related systems that contain valuable information and function properly. Blockchain can consume a wealth of resources, especially at start-up, and some managers believe that that the time and money spent are not worth the return-on-investment. They choose to implement other traceability systems that get the job done with minimal resource consumption.

Based on the above advantages and disadvantages, leaders of manufacturing companies will need to fully understand the pros and cons of blockchain before making it a part of their supply chain monitoring process. This leads us to the next section which discusses the future of this intriguing technology.

Future

Without a crystal ball, it is difficult to determine who will use blockchain in the future. However, it can be said with confidence that many business leaders will take a serious look at it because it has the potential to do things that competing forms of technology are not able to do. That being said, the following are areas of manufacturing where blockchain has the greatest potential:

Cyber security

This area of manufacturing where blockchain has potential should not come as a surprise to anyone since security is a known advantage of the technology. However, blockchain will move well past traceability into financial areas such as accounts payable and accounts receivable. It will make financial transactions more accurate and transparent, and it will also speed up the process; thereby saving time and money.

Transportation

Transportation, which includes warehousing, distribution, and trucking, will be part of blockchain's future for manufacturers. While every aspect of the supply chain could potentially be affected by blockchain technology, transportation stands out on its own because it allows manufacturers to store and ship products without involving costly third parties. Time and money will be saved, and those savings will make manufacturing leaders happy.

Employee benefits

Major headaches for leaders of manufacturing companies include the benefit packages that they provide to their employees. Healthcare, in particular, continues to rise in cost and it appears this trend will continue in the future. Blockchain can help stabilize health care costs by improving data security, speeding the sharing of information between medical institutions and patients, and verifying that information is accurate. In short, lower costs for medical care professionals will prevent the sharp price increases that manufacturers have been continuously experiencing.

Plant expansion

As noted earlier, blockchain assures the accuracy of financial transactions while speeding up processes and procedures. This advantage will translate into savings in many other areas including the acquisition of physical space for plant expansion. The transparency of real estate transactions will prevent errors and fraud while eliminating the need for paper records. Manufacturers need space to produce more products, and blockchain will expedite the purchasing of that space while assuring proper documentation is in order.

Summary

Blockchain technology is not new, but it has never been as popular as it is today due to the need for accurate, time-stamped, and irreversible data. Manufacturers are particularly interested in this technology due to the length and complexity of their supply chains and the fact that their customers are always demanding more in terms of information.

Blockchain technology is used by many different businesses, and this book explores its use in manufacturing. It introduces blockchain, describes its function, exemplifies its applications, identifies its strengths and weaknesses, and predicts its future. The text is informational and educational, and it is written for easy understanding at any reader level.

Congratulations! You now understand more about blockchain technology for manufacturers...a topic of interest that continues to grow in popularity.

Risk Management
in Organizations
A Basic Introduction

Allison Shearsett and Louis Bevoc

Published by
NutriNiche System LLC

For information contact:
info@nutriniche.com

Louis Bevoc books...simple explanations of complex subjects

Introduction

Organizations experience a wide variety of risks, and leaders need to make decisions based on the potential rewards or consequences of those risks. They do this by implementing programs known as risk management. These programs are designed to reduce uncertainty in organizations when the effects of something that might happen are unknown. This is important because negative effects can compromise the goals and objectives of organizations...and they can even lead to businesses shutting down.

Uncertain times have led many companies to stop forecasting or predicting their future. Economic downfalls, terrorism threats, environmental concerns, and political changes have all impacted the way business is conducted, and this has led to leaders being more discrete about their short-term and long-term plans. Uncertainties have also resulted in leaders choosing to focus more on risk management then they have ever done in the past. They try to identify the most significant risks in their organizations and act accordingly with programs designed to reduce or eliminate them.

Essentially, any actions that reduce or eliminate risk fall under the umbrella of risk management. These actions help organizations secure their future by warding off potential problems before they occur. Risk management allows companies to make business decisions with confidence, and it also provides options when potential problems become reality. Organizations that make decisions without evaluating risk are gambling...and that gambling can lead to their demise.

Risk management programs also play a big role in protecting organizations from potential catastrophes. These programs are put in place for decision making that identifies potential danger and works toward preventing or eliminating it. In short, they help organizations achieve goals and objectives while controlling the risks involved.

Now that you understand the concept of risk management, let's move to a discussion on the six basic steps involved.

Six steps

Essentially, risk management programs involve the six steps listed below. A meat processing company is used as an example for each step.

Assemble

This step involves assembling the risk management team. Care needs to be taken when selecting people because there should be a mixture of job responsibilities and personalities that allow the team to identify and analyze risk from multiple perspectives without bias. Work experience is also important because veteran employees typically have knowledge that is worth its weight in gold...and new employees often make suggestions that were previously never considered. The goal of the selection process is to make sure the team is heterogeneous so members do not all think the same. Diversity is the key to assessing risk in any situation.

Example

A meat processing company decides to implement a risk management program. They start by assembling a risk management team that consists of the plant manager, quality manager, sales manager, distribution manager, and office manager.

The plant manager and quality manager have been with the organization for more than 15 years. They have seen the company go through growth phases, and they also understand what they need to do when sales slow and times get tough. They have a very good grasp of the processes, policies, and procedures that are utilized for manufacturing meat products. In short, their experience is very valuable because they understand many of the risks involved when running a production facility.

The sales manager does not fully understand plant operations, but she is well aware of customer needs. She has only been with the company for six months, but prior to this job, she worked for a competitor for seven years. She sees risks involved with product being out in the field...particularly those that involve food safety because the last company she worked for had a product recall due to bacterial contamination. This experience causes her to perceive the risk of recall as very serious.

The distribution manager has been with the meat processing company for over three years. He understands finished product storage, inventory, and transportation. He perceives product loss, damage, and theft as the biggest risks in his department because he has the unfortunate experience of seeing all three of these problems occur while product is stored or transported to other locations. His finished product perception makes him a valuable member of the risk management team.

The office manager understands record storage, customer service, accounting, and payroll. She realizes embezzlement and other white-collar theft are potential issues. She also knows the risks involved with calculating employee hours worked, paying invoices, or collecting money owed to the company. She views risks from an administrative standpoint, and her perception adds diversity to the risk management team.

Identify

This is where risks are realized. Each team member identifies and documents the risks that they see in their organization. Their perception is valuable because everyone perceives things differently.

This procedure should not take place in meetings because (1) some team members are more dominant than others and (2) there is potential for groupthink. Each member needs to think independently and document the risks they determine to be important. This asynchronous process gives all members flexibility so they can fit their thinking into their routine work schedules.

Example

The risk management team members at the meat processing company think about risks from their perspectives and identify them as follows:

Plant manager

Risks identified: power, productivity, nature, inventory, staffing, attendance

More specifically:

- *Power* refers to the risk of power outages
- *Productivity* refers to the risk of losing manufacturing productivity
- *Nature* refers to the risk of natural disasters (tornados, high winds, lightning strikes, earthquakes, etc.)
- *Inventory* refers to the risk of overstocking or understocking raw materials
- *Staffing* refers to the risk of having the right people for the jobs
- *Attendance* refers to the risk of people not showing up for their jobs (due to strikes, sickness, vacations, etc.)

Quality manager

Risks identified: allergens, bacteria, metal, chemicals, flavor, appearance

More specifically:

- *Allergens* refer to the risk of exposing people to ingredients that give them allergic reactions
- *Bacteria* refers to the risk of product being contaminated with disease causing bacteria
- *Metal* refers to the risk of product being contaminated with metal
- *Chemicals* refers to the risk of product being contaminated with chemicals
- *Flavor* refers to the risk of products having an off taste
- *Appearance* refers to the risk of color and shape being wrong

Sales manager

Risks identified: product recalls, price, new products, service, quality, availability

More specifically:

- *Product recalls* refer to the risk of product being recalled back to the company for consumer safety once it has been shipped
- *Price* refers to the risk of costumers not buying product because it costs too much
- *New products* refer to the risk of the company not producing the new products necessary to compete
- *Service* refers to the risk of customers not being happy with the service provided to them
- *Quality* refers to the risk of product not meeting acceptable quality standards

Distribution manager

Risks identified: transportation, delivery vehicles, drivers, accidents, inventory, nature

More specifically:

- *Transpiration* refers to the risk of lost or damaged product during transportation
- *Delivery vehicles* refers to the risk of delivery vehicles not running properly when needed
- *Drivers* refers to the risk of driver shortages
- *Accidents* refers to the risk of drivers getting into accidents
- *Inventory* refers to the risk of inventory being inaccurate, stolen, or lost.
- *Nature* refers to the risk of bad weather that prevents delivery of products

Office manager

Risks identified: customer satisfaction, employee ethics, theft, attendance, payables, receivables

More specifically:

- *Customer satisfaction* refers to the risk of customers not being satisfied with products or service
- *Employee ethics* refers to the risk of unethical employee actions
- *Theft* refers to the risk of white-collar theft
- *Attendance* refers to the risk of employees missing excessive time at work
- *Payables* refers to the risk of suppliers not being paid
- *Receivables* refers to the risk of customers not paying their bills

Analyze

Now the team gets together to categorize the risks that have been submitted by individual members. Some risks overlap and can be combined in the same category, others need their own separate category, and still, others are eliminated. These categories define the type of risk and its potential impact on organizational goals and objectives. They also create a solid structure that helps facilitate the next step of the process (evaluate).

Example

The risk management team members at the meat processing company reduce the identified risks to the following categories:

Natural disasters

This includes inclement weather, tornadoes, earthquakes, lightning, flooding, snowdrifts, and flooding.

Food safety

This includes product recalls, product spoilage, and product contamination.

Customer satisfaction

This includes price, delivery, order fulfillment, and quality.

Employee attendance

This includes delivery personnel, production personnel, and replacement personnel.

Finances

This includes payables and receivables.

Employee ethics

This includes unethical and illegal employee actions.

Inventory

This includes shortages and overages of finished product or raw materials

Evaluate

After risks have been categorized, it is time to rank them in order of importance. Typically this is done by evaluating each risk for its potential to occur and consequences that can result. Some risks are important enough to be quickly addressed in the next step while others can be moved to the backburner.

This step is sometimes considered the most difficult because inaccurate evaluations can lead to unanticipated problems...essentially defeating the purpose of the risk management team. However, there is a need for an order of importance, and evaluation addresses that need.

Example

The risk management team members at the meat processing company establish the following order of importance:

Employee attendance

Why? Employee attendance is a threat virtually every day. It is hard to get everyone to show up for work, and productivity is hindered on a fairly regular basis. For this reason, employee attendance ranks first on the list of important risks.

Food safety

Why? The meat processing company has not had a recall, and they have only had one complaint of a customer getting sick. However, the potential is there and the consequences could be devastating. Allergens are also present in the plant, and there is a risk that they could contaminate products without being listed in the ingredient statements.

Customer satisfaction

Why? Sales are critical for the meat processing company. A large reduction in sales volume could risk the survival of the organization.

Finances

Why? Vendors must be paid for their services or they will discontinue being vendors, and the meat processing company must get paid to have money to operate. Based on this, financial risk potentially threatens the well-being of the organization.

Inventory

Why? Raw material and finished product inventory outages affect the fulfillment of customer orders, and inventory overages tie up money that could be used elsewhere. There is a risk with inventory, but it is not major.

Natural disasters

Why? Tornadoes and flooding are threats that can occur with little or no warning. These weather disasters are a longshot, but they do present a minimum risk.

Employee ethics

Why? Unethical and illegal concerns have not been a problem in the past, but the potential for their occurrence does exist on a small level. For this reason, employee ethics receives the lowest ranking in terms of risk importance.

Address

Once risks have been categorized and ranked, it is time to address those that have been determined to be the most important. This is commonly referred to as response planning, and it is where the treatment begins. This treatment involves reducing the risks to acceptable levels using strategic planning and contingency planning. The goal is to minimize the probability of negative risks (strategic planning) while determining ways to address the problems that result when risks become reality (contingency planning).

Unfortunately, contingency planning often faces two major obstacles. These obstacles are:

Motivation

Contingency planning is essentially a backup plan that goes into effect if the strategic plan is not successful. Many risk management teams put so much time and effort into their strategic plan that they think it will be successful regardless of the circumstances. They simply believe that they will not need a contingency plan, so they are not motivated to create one.

Urgency

In reality, there is a low probability of a situation that will require a contingency plan. Yes, there are circumstances that create a crisis, but those circumstances are viewed as few and far between....so contingency planning moves to the bottom of the list in terms of importance. When something is a low importance priority, it tends to never get done properly because there is no sense of urgency.

Example

The risk management team members at the meat processing company establish the following risk reduction measures as part of their strategic plan:

Employee attendance

On the job training is conducted at the plant, and this reduces the risk of employee missing work due to injuries. Job rotation is also ongoing; thereby allowing employees to learn each other's jobs and function as backups.

Food safety

A HACCP program is in place to address food safety in the plant. It pinpoints critical areas of meat processing to assure meat is safe when it leaves the plant. Additionally, all employees are educated on food safety and food defense. They are trained when they start with the meat processing company and on an annual basis.

Customer satisfaction

Surveys are sent to customers to assess their satisfaction. These surveys allow respondents to provide detailed information about why they are not happy.

Finances

All accounting and office personnel undergo initial and annual financial training specifically geared toward the meat processing company. This assures fewer mistakes will be made in the office.

Inventory

Employees conduct a month-end inventory to reduce the risk of error, and weekly meetings are held between manufacturing, distribution, and purchasing personnel to discuss shortages and overages.

Natural disasters

The plant roof is inspected annually for damage, and the plant walls are constructed to withstand 70 MPH winds. This assures building security under severe weather conditions.

Employee ethics

A written ethics policy is given to all employees when they are hired. They must (1) pass a written test that shows they understand the policy and (2) sign off that they are in possession of the policy.

As part of their contingency plant, the risk management team members at the meat processing company establish the following to reduce problems that occur when risks become reality:

Employee attendance

A contract is established with a temporary staffing firm if the company experiences employee shortages. This firm can provide up to 100 employees within one hour of being contacted by the meat processing company.

Food safety

Mock recalls are conducted to assure all affected product can be recalled. These recalls trace all raw materials to original sources and all finished products to end-users. A law firm has also been contracted to handle interaction with the government and others if a recall becomes public.

Customer satisfaction

A policy is in place that refunds customers the product purchase price if they are not satisfied with for any reason. Customers merely need to show proof of purchase, and they will be promptly refunded.

Finances

Internal audits are performed for all major financial discrepancies, and a contracted CPA firm is available for consultation.

Inventory

Internal investigations are performed for all major inventory discrepancies, and a contracted CPA firm is available for consultation.

Natural disasters

Local authorities (police, fire, utilities) are contacted to assess the situation and recommend a course of action. These individuals are trained in natural disaster response, and they have access to resources that are not available to the meat processing company.

Employee ethics

Internal investigations are performed for all unethical or illegal activities, and a contracted law firm is available for consultation.

Monitor

At this point, the risk management team has identified, analyzed, evaluated, and addressed important risks in their organization. However, the program still needs to be monitored to assure that it is working properly.

In this step, questions need to be asked. Is the program working as intended? Are the established controls still effective? Will the established controls be effective in the future? What are the weak points? What needs to be changed? If the program has been successful, then it can be left as is without change. However, if the program has failed or the future points towards its failure, then changes need to be made.

Example

The risk management team members at the meat processing company monitor the program as follows:

Employee attendance

Employee attendance is monitored using an employee attendance system that has a two-fold effect. It rewards employees with good attendance and disciplines those with poor attendance. Additionally, the fill-rate of the temporary employer is tracked. If the fill-rate falls below 80 percent, then other temporary employment services are explored as an option.

Food safety

Trends are tracked for all food safety deviations from the HACCP plan. Established trends require the meat processing company to make changes to processes and procedures to prevent future reoccurrences.

Customer satisfaction

Data from customer surveys is collected and analyzed for trends. Any negative trends require changes to be made to prevent reoccurrences.

Finances

> All accounts payable and accounts receivable errors are documented. If a trend develops, then action is taken to determine why that trend occurred and how it can be prevented from reoccurring.

Inventory

> Inventory outages and overages are tracked and documented. If a trend develops, then meetings are held to determine why the problem occurred and how to prevent a reoccurrence.

Natural disasters

> All damage is documented on a list. Management reviews the list to find weak points that can be made stronger to prevent a recurrence.

Employee ethics

> Unethical employee behavior is documented and disciplinary action is taken to prevent a reoccurrence. This discipline can involve employee termination and/or legal action.

Now you understand the premise of a risk management program and the basic steps involved in establishing that program and putting it into action. Let's expand on this discussion in the next section by describing the two major types of risk management.

Types

This section simplifies two rather complex types of risk management so they can be understood by most people. These types are quantitative and qualitative, and they are broken down as follows:

Quantitative

Quantitative risk management determines the cost of catastrophic situations by establishing the probability of occurrence and the potential consequences resulting from that occurrence. It classifies and evaluates the impact of problems on organizations and their employees. In short, it determines the cost of lost productivity, replacement of assets, and damaged reputation using statistical analysis. For example, the meat processing risk management team might use a continuous variable commonly known as return on investment (ROI) to determine the standard deviation (variance) of a financial risk. First, they identify the threats that produce the biggest estimated losses, and then they determine appropriate measures to reduce those losses.

An advantage of quantitative risk management is the results are objective. Personal bias is not a factor because the statistical analysis is used to determine risk. However, a disadvantage of quantitative risk management is the complexity of the process. The calculation of results can be difficult and cumbersome.

Qualitative

Qualitative risk management does not utilize statistical analysis and is therefore used by many small organizations. It uses relative values to determine potential loss if a problem occurs. In short, it awards scores for the probability of problematic situations and the need for action to minimize the risk involved. For example, the meat processing company is located in rural Kansas. The risk management team might evaluate the probability of a hurricane as insignificant and the need to take action to reduce the risk as very minor. Along the same lines, they might evaluate the probability of employees missing work as very likely and the need to take action to reduce risk as major.

The advantages of qualitative risk management include ease of calculation and implementation. The method is relatively simple to understand and implement in most organizations. However, a major disadvantage is personal bias. Lack of statistical analyses allows employees the ability to manipulate results based on their perceptions of situations.

Quantitative and qualitative types of risk management have both experienced success and failure, but each type has a goal of identifying risks and reducing or eliminating them. That being said, there must be ways to improve risk management in general...and that is why improvement is the focus of the next section.

Improving

Risk management programs provide many benefits to organizations. This makes sense because if they were not advantageous, then they would not be implemented. However, these programs are not foolproof and they can always be improved. Suggestions for improvement include:

Follow the program

Some risk management teams try to implement risk management programs without following the six basic steps. These steps are essential for the success of risk management because they promote continuous improvement of predictive power. For example, the risk management team at the meat processing company might decide not to evaluate the importance of each risk that has been categorized. They believe all risks are equally important, so there is no point in evaluating them individually. This might appear to be a rational decision, but it is a mistake because equal risk importance is not the reality of their situation. It is much more likely for employees to miss work than it is for bad weather to damage the building. Ranking these two risks as identical is doing an injustice to the organization in terms of preparing for problems that might occur in the future.

Define roles

Risk management is dependent on a team, and each member needs to contribute in a unique way. If two members have the same responsibilities, then the team is not performing at a peak level and success will be negatively impacted. For example, if three members of the meat processing company's team are all assessing risk from a production standpoint, then the overall team effectiveness is reduced because other areas of the operation are not considered. Team members must have a goal of increasing predictive power for all organizational risks...and this starts by defining roles.

Ask open-ended questions

Many questions asked by team members are closed-ended and they fail to produce the detailed answers required to create a successful risk management program. For example, the president of the meat processing company might ask the office manager if she believes white-collar embezzlement is a risk. This question will get a "yes" or "no" answer, but it could generate much more valuable information if the president asked the office manager to explain why she does or does not see while collar embezzlement as a risk.

Principle not position

This is related to the "define roles" suggestion discussed earlier in this section. Risk management personnel need to focus on "principle not position" by doing what is best for everyone involved. For example, individual team members at the meat processing company need to step back to view the organization as a whole. Risks need to be identified based on the good of the organization, not the department or the individual. This can be difficult, but it is possible and it will achieve the best results.

Leadership commitment

This suggestion is rather simple. Commitment to a risk management program needs to start at the top of the organization...but unfortunately, this is not always the case. In many instances, commitment is only found at the lower levels of organizational hierarchies. This creates situations where employees are not encouraged to move forward with thoughts and ideas, and their motivation to implement and maintain a risk management program fades over time. For example, if the president of the meat processing company does not show interest in the risk management program, then the team will follow his lead the program will never be useful. In short, risk management programs without leadership commitment do not have the necessary support to take root and prosper.

Realize opinion limitations

It must always be remembered that risk management is based on opinions...and everyone on the risk management team has an opinion. Their opinions are shaped by their education and experiences...and those opinions can be bias. Diverse make-up of team members helps prevent similar thinking and opens the door to new ideas, but it does little to change opinions. For example, the meat processing company put together a fairly diverse team. However, all of these people harbor feelings that result in their individual preferences. In this sense, opinions are a limiting factor of risk management because they are naturally slanted toward personal thoughts, experiences, ideas, and concerns.

Another problem with opinions is the fact that it is impossible to predict who is right and who is wrong. If organizations knew the risks they were going to face in the future, they would not need a risk management team. They would simply prepare based on what they know is going to happen. For example, If the leadership at the meat processing company knew that the only risk they will face in the future is food safety, then they would forego the risk management program and focus their efforts on preventing food safety problems. In short, risk assessment is about the future...and the future cannot be predicted with 100 percent assurance based on people's opinions.

Now that you understand some ways of improving risk management, it is time to move on to the last section that discusses the future of this interesting concept.

Future

What does the future look like for risk management? This is an interesting question because risk management is about the future...so it is essentially asking what something that predicts the future will look like in the future. Regardless of the irony involved with this question, the answer is "very good." However, there will be some changes due to the impact of a few factors.

The following factors will impact the future of risk management:

Regulatory agencies

Not surprisingly, regulatory intervention is going to increase in the future. Government agencies will have goals of protecting consumers, and they will achieve those goals by implementing new rules and regulations. When this happens, organizations will find themselves facing even more risks. Those risks will need to be reduced, and that reduction will be accomplished using risk management. In short, regulatory agencies will continue to make changes...and risk management will address those changes.

Technology

Technology impacts virtually every aspect of an organization. This impact is often for the better, but it does lead to increased risk. For example, a technological advancement that makes something easier has a risk of failure that can leave an organization helpless. Along the same lines, complex technology runs the risk of employees not understanding how it works. Technological risks will certainly be present in the future, but they will be minimized if organizations utilize risk management. This means the advent of technology will lead to an increase in risk management programs for organizations all over the world.

Globalization

Global competition has become the norm for many organizations. They sell their products and services internationally, and they have no intention of changing this strategy in the future. In fact, more and more companies will jump on the global bandwagon because there is great potential for growth and expansion. However, global competition brings about changes in social norms, politics, ethics, and the environment that create new risks. These risks need to be reduced...and risk management achieves that reduction. Risk management programs will need to modify their approach, but they will help prevent many global risks from becoming reality.

Culture

People in management typically base their decisions on the values and beliefs of their employers. Those decisions help some organizations grow and prosper, but they also drive other organizations out of business. It is impossible to predict with 100 percent accuracy whether future decisions will be right or wrong, but it is a known fact that those decisions will create risk....and that risk needs to be addressed. In the future, the culture of organizations will create a risk that will be minimized by risk management programs.

Summary

Risk management is an appealing concept due to the uncertainty that exists in many organizations. It is more important today than it ever was in the past, and that importance appears to be growing. Based on its popularity, risk management is taking center stage in the thought processes of leaders all over the world.

This book focuses on risk management in organizations. It introduces six basic steps for development and implementation, describes major types of methodology, suggests methods of improvement, and examines the future of this interesting concept. The text is informational and educational, and it is written for easy reader understanding at all levels.

Congratulations! You now understand more about risk management...a useful program for predicting and protecting the future of organizations.